6 Qualities of the Believers

By
Shaykh Mufti Saiful Islām

JKN Publications

First Published in March 2020

ISBN 978-1-909114-54-8

British Library Cataloguing in Publication Data
A catalogue record for this book is available from the British Library.

Publisher's Note:

Every care and attention has been put into the production of this book. If however, you find any errors they are our own, for which we seek Allāh's ﷻ for-
giveness and the reader's pardon.

Published by:

JKN Publications
118 Manningham Lane
Bradford
West Yorkshire
BD8 7JF
United Kingdom

t: +44 (0) 1274 308 456 | w: www.jkn.org.uk | e: info@jkn.org.uk

Book Title: 6 Qualities of the Believers

Author: Shaykh Mufti Saiful Islām

Printed by Mega Printing in Turkey

"In the Name of Allāh, the Most Beneficent,
the Most Merciful"

Contents

Introduction …… 5

Quality 1: Prayer … …… … … … … … … … … … … … … … … ….. 7

The Stages of Khushū. … … … … … … … … … … … … … … … …. 8

Quality 2: Avoiding Futile Things … … … … … … … … … … … 11

Quality 3: Zakāt … … … … … … … … … … … … … … … … … …. 12

Quality 4: Chastity … … … … … … … … … … … … … … … … … 16

Importance of Marriage … … … … … … … … … … … … … … ….. 17

Quality 5: Fulfilling Promises … … … … … … … … … … … … … 19

Quality 6: Salāh … … … … … … … … … … … … … … … … … …. 24

Reward of the Successful … … … … … … … … … … … … … … … 26

Introduction

All praises be to Allāh ﷻ, the Lord of the worlds and may peace and blessings be showered upon the Final Messenger, Muhammad ﷺ, upon his noble Companions ﷺ and upon those who follow their noble lifestyles until the final hour.

Respected readers, do you want to be successful in this life and the Hereafter? The fact that you have prompted yourself to pick up this book and read, is an indication that the answer is *yes*. Or perhaps, you were not aware of the contents and purpose of this book and hence, eternal success wasn't the first thing on your mind. Nonetheless, it is easy to turn your attention towards this objective right now.

The fact is that we all crave, desire, wish and endeavour for success, in this life and the Hereafter. So let us embark on this path by following the commandments of Allāh ﷻ and His Noble Messenger Muhammad ﷺ, which will gain us close proximity to Allāh ﷻ and inevitably lead to our success. The hope is that this book will assist us in our goal of achieving such success, so let us read, learn and implement Inshā-Allāh.

In the opening verses of the 18th Juzz, Allāh ﷻ mentions who the *truly* successful ones are and the ones that will attain success in this world and the Hereafter.

قَدۡ أَفۡلَحَ الۡمُؤۡمِنُوۡنَ

Indeed, the true believers are the successful. (23:1)

قَدۡ in the Arabic language emphasises certainty. It indicates towards something which is verily going to happen.

الۡمُؤۡمِنُوۡنَ are those people who are the *true* believers.

Allāh ﷻ mentions 6 qualities in portrayal of these people. Let us read these 6 qualities carefully and try to inculcate them into our lives, Inshā-Allāh.

May Allāh ﷻ accept this work, bless the readers with a purified heart and make us from amongst the closest friends of Allāh ﷻ in this world and the Hereafter. May Allāh ﷻ make us all sincere seekers of the True Path and make this book a means of benefit for the masses and the scholars of this Ummah. Āmīn!

Quality 1: Prayer

Allāh ﷻ says:

اَلَّذِيْنَ هُمْ فِيْ صَلَاتِهِمْ خَاشِعُوْنَ

They who are during their prayer humbly submissive (23:2)

The first quality of the truly successful are those who are genuinely devoted in their Salāh. They have perfect devotion, dedication, attention and focus towards their prayers. Over here, Allāh ﷻ is highlighting the importance of Salāh. He expresses its significance by mentioning that, for a person to be successful, he must be regular, consistent and punctual in his Salāh.

In another verse, Allāh ﷻ mentions regarding Salāh:

اَلَّذِيْنَ يُقِيْمُوْنَ الصَّلَاةَ وَمِمَّا رَزَقْنَاهُمْ يُنْفِقُوْنَ

The ones who establish prayer, and from what We have provided them, they spend. (8:3)

يُقِيْمُوْنَ comes from the word إِقَامَة which means, 'to establish'. When we *establish* something, we bring it into existence in a firm and strong manner. Consider the example of a person who establishes a building. The first priority of the building would be in ensuring its' foundations and basis are solid and firm. Without this crucial step, the building would not hold up. In a similar way, Salāh will be deeply established when a person performs it in the proper way, that is, by practicing all the Farā'idh (compulsory acts), Sunan (Sunnah acts) and Mustahabbāt (virtuous acts) which have been explained to us by our beloved Nabi 🕮.

The Stages of Khushū

Khushū refers to the devotion a person possesses during Salāh. According to the Fuqahā (scholars), Khushū has different stages:

<u>The first stage</u>

The first stage is also the one which is Fardh (compulsory). This is when the Salāh is initiated. Whenever any of us start our Salāh and offer the first Takbīr (Takbīr Tahrīmah); we bear in mind which Salāh we are intending to read. This is the least amount of Khushū that is compulsory for a person. If a person doesn't even know which Salāh he is reading, then his Khushū and Salāh is void. So, when he has recited "Allāhu-Akbar", and is aware of which Salāh he is performing, then this is sufficient. If after this, his mind happens to roam around, his Salāh will still be accepted because the Fardh was completed.

<u>The second stage</u>

This stage of Khushū entails a person performing his Salāh, completing all the different positions whilst knowing what he is reading. His mind is present at the time of performing the various postures.

The third stage

The final stage is the highest stage. The ultimate Khushū is when a person, throughout his Salāh, from the beginning till the very end, his ultimate focus is towards Allāh ﷻ. He is aware of everything he is reading.

It is mentioned in Hadīth-e-Jibrīl, that once Sayyidunā Jibrīl ﵇ asked the Prophet ﷺ: مَا الْإِحْسَانُ (What is Ihsān?) The Prophet ﷺ replied:

اَلْإِحْسَانُ أَنْ تَعْبُدَ اللهَ كَأَنَّكَ تَرَاهُ فَإِنْ لَّمْ تَكُنْ تَرَاهُ فَإِنَّهُ يَرَاكَ

(That you worship Allāh as though you can see Him, if you cannot see Him then remember and keep in your mind that Allāh ﷻ can see you). (Bukhāri & Muslim)

Once Shaykh Ashraf Ali Thānwi ﵀ was asked, how can we create Khushū in our Salāh? Shaykh replied, that when a person is performing his Salāh he should be like a person who does not know his Qur'ān properly. If he reads the Qur'ān in this way, whilst reciting every word and verse, he will be thinking about the next one. Thus, he will have full concentration on his words and on the verse that is going to be recited. Likewise, in Salāh, every posture made and every verse recited should be done with full concentration and total awareness. When a person prays like this, then they have adopted true Khushū in their Salāh.

What a beautiful answer Hakīmul Ummah ﷺ has given. This is one of the reasons why Shaykh Ashraf Ali Thānwi ﷺ was known as the 'Physician of the Ummah'.

Shaykh Zakariyya ﷺ says, that when a person performs his Salāh, he should be like a slave who has ran away from his master and now the master has caught him. He is guilty. He has been disobedient. Now how should he stand in front of his Master?

Subhān-Allāh! What devotion and dedication these people used to have in their Salāh! May Allāh ﷻ grant us all the ability to pray our Salāh with complete devotion. Āmīn!

Quality 2: Avoiding Futile Things

وَالَّذِيْنَ هُمْ عَنِ اللَّغْوِ مُعْرِضُوْنَ

Those who from futile things they move away (23:3)

The second quality of the successful is that they move away from anything which does not concern them. They do not intrude or interfere with matters and nor do they cause problems with them. The significance of this is clearly mentioned in the following Hadīth:

مِنْ حُسْنِ إِسْلَامِ الْمَرْءِ تَرْكُهُ مَا لَا يَعْنِيْهِ

"Part of a person's goodness in Islām is his leaving alone of that which does not concern him." (Tirmizi & Ahmad)

In another verse, where Allāh ﷻ speaks about the qualities of the worshippers of Ar-Rahmān, He says:

وَإِذَا مَرُّوْا بِاللَّغْوِ مَرُّوْا كِرَامًا

When they pass by any futile things, they pass in an honourable way (25:72)

'In an honourable way' meaning, they do not become engrossed in such things. Thus, it is said that when a person is passing by something which is wrong, he lowers his gaze and hastens his pace. So, this is the quality of the pious people - وَالَّذِيْنَ هُمْ عَنِ اللَّغْوِ مُعْرِضُوْنَ

The word اَللَّغْوُ refers to anything which is not beneficial. Unfortunately today, this is the biggest problem we have. We waste our time with all those non-essential matters. Even with regards to speech we should be extremely cautious. If something is unnecessary, then let us keep quiet and if something is necessary, then speak. Unfortunately, our *everything* is excessive! Our eating, drinking, talking and even our intermingling goes beyond the moderation limit. So my advice, respected readers, is that when you come across any kind of اَللَّغْوُ, then *completely* ignore it. May Allāh ﷻ protect us from anything اَللَّغْوُ. Āmīn!

Quality 3: Zakāt

وَالَّذِيْنَ هُمْ لِلزَّكَاةِ فَاعِلُوْنَ

And regarding Zakāt, they fulfil the Zakāt (23:4)

Zakāt is the third quality of the successful people specifically mentioned by Allāh ﷻ. Subhān-Allāh! We think about Zakāt only in the month of Ramadhān. The question is, what about the remaining eleven months? What will the state of the poor people be? This is why we need to continuously pay Zakāt and give Sadaqah frequently. Allāh ﷻ has placed great wisdom behind the act of Zakāt; the more the effort, the less you give.

In another verse, Allāh ﷻ says:

وَهُوَ الَّذِيٓ أَنشَأَ جَنَّٰتٍ مَّعۡرُوشَٰتٍ وَغَيۡرَ مَعۡرُوشَٰتٍ وَٱلنَّخۡلَ وَٱلزَّرۡعَ مُخۡتَلِفًا أُكُلُهُ وَٱلزَّيۡتُونَ وَٱلرُّمَّانَ مُتَشَٰبِهًا وَغَيۡرَ مُتَشَٰبِهٍ ۚ كُلُوا۟ مِن ثَمَرِهِۦٓ إِذَآ أَثۡمَرَ وَءَاتُوا۟ حَقَّهُۥ يَوۡمَ حَصَادِهِۦ ۖ وَلَا تُسۡرِفُوٓا۟ ۚ إِنَّهُۥ لَا يُحِبُّ ٱلۡمُسۡرِفِينَ

And He it is Who causes gardens to grow, (both) trellised and untrellised, and palm trees and crops of different (kinds of) food and olives and pomegranates, similar and dissimilar. Eat of (each of) its fruit when it yields and give its due (Zakāt) on the day of its harvest. And be not excessive. Indeed, He does not like those who commit excess. (6:141)

Where Allāh ﷻ says:

وَءَاتُوا۟ حَقَّهُۥ يَوۡمَ حَصَادِهِ

and give its due (Zakāt) on the day of its harvest

Under this verse, the scholars of Tafsīr mention that there are different categories, Subhān-Allāh.

Consider the situation of a person who purchases a house, and just so happens to find treasure under its cellar! If the person who previously owned the house admits to being unaware of the treasure, then there is a ruling in regards to the new found treasure. According to the Sharī'ah, the poor and needy would be entitled to 20% of it, whilst the remaining bulk of the treasure, 80%, belongs to the person who found it! Subhān-Allāh! Just imagine, this wealth that the person did hardly anything to achieve, its majority is given to him, and at the same time, the poor and needy are maintained.

Example two; a person owns land by which, its cultivation has been achieved through nature, such as rain water and the sunlight. In this case, 10% of the harvest will be given for Zakāt, as very little hard work was done to maintain the harvest. However, if the person uses his own cattle and equipment, then only 5% is due.

And regarding that which a person has worked all year round in, from the profit (after subtracting all necessary expenditure etc), only 2.5% is to be given as Zakāt. *Only* 2.5%. Let's just observe the system of Islām, the harder the work, the less you give! Unfortunately, these days it seems that we cant even give that 2.5%.

Allāh ﷻ says:

كَىْ لَا يَكُوْنَ دُوْلَةً بَيْنَ الْأَغْنِيَآءِ مِنْكُمْ

So that this wealth may not remain as hoarded riches with the wealthy among you. (59:7)

That it (the wealth) should be continuously rotating, so that it does not remain amongst the wealthy people only. Tragically, the system that we have in the world is that the rich become richer at the expense of the poor, who become even more in need.

Umar Ibn Abdul Azīz ﷺ became the Caliph in the year 99AH and passed away during 101AH. He only ruled for two years, yet, in this small amount of time, he transformed the land. Subhān-Allāh, it is said that in his time people used to come with Zakāt but there was nobody to give it to! When people were assumed to be eligible for Zakāt, they used to say 'Alhamdulillāh, we have got enough.' There was not a single person who was entitled to Zakāt because he implemented the system of the rich giving to the poor and thus, the poor had enough.

Subhān-Allāh, this is how practical and beneficial the Islamic system is to society. If we were to utilize the Islamic system in every aspect, whether it is do with crime and punishment, financial dealings, social life, worship, or even living amongst those who practice a different faith, everything would be compatible and cohesive, because Islām has taught us all this.

So, respected readers, returning back to the verse:

وَالَّذِيْنَ هُمْ لِلزَّكُوةِ فَاعِلُوْنَ

The word فَاعِلُوْنَ - in Arabic Grammar terms, is an Ism Fā'il, which denotes *continuity*. It does not just apply only in the month of Ramadhān, rather, the successful ones *continuously* give. They don't stop at any moment.

May Allāh ﷻ keep us steadfast and firm on our obligation of Zakāt, and also on our Sadaqāt. Āmīn!

Quality 4: Chastity

وَالَّذِيْنَ هُمْ لِفُرُوْجِهِمْ حَافِظُوْنَ

And they who guard their private parts (23:5)

The fourth quality of the successful people is that they safeguard their chastity. They do not indulge in adultery, fornication or other immoral acts.

<u>The difference between fornication and adultery</u>
Fornication is when unmarried individuals partake in illicit relationships. Adultery is when a married individual/s are having extra marital affairs. Both are completely Harām.

Another breach of chastity would be a person (Na'ūdhubillāh) committing homosexual acts. Or (Na'ūdhubillāh) a person fulfilling his/her desires through masturbation. All of these things have been classified as Harām. Hence, to fulfil the sexual desires through any of these means would be completely Harām and major sins.

In the next verse, Allāh ﷻ mentions the correct and Halāl way of how to utilize and fulfil the natural, carnal desires. Allāh ﷻ has given us the Halāl system *and* the Harām system. They are both present in front of us. It is for *us* to choose. Allāh ﷻ has granted man intellect to be able to distinguish between right and wrong. So, He is saying that the Ḥalāl way to fulfil your desires is through Nikāh. The Ḥarām system is without marriage.

Importance of Marriage

إِلَّا عَلَىٰٓ أَزْوَاجِهِمْ أَوْ مَا مَلَكَتْ أَيْمَانُهُمْ فَإِنَّهُمْ غَيْرُ مَلُوْمِيْنَ

Except from their wives or those their right hands possess, for indeed, they will not be blamed (23:6)

A major problem we face today is that we have failed to understand the importance and need of marriage. Subḥān-Allāh, the significance of marriage can be seen just by one Ḥadīth of Nabi Karīm ﷺ, when he said,

إِذَا تَزَوَّجَ الْعَبْدُ فَقَدِ اسْتَكْمَلَ نِصْفَ الدِّيْنِ فَلْيَتَّقِ اللّٰهَ فِي النِّصْفِ الْبَاقِيْ

"When a servant gets married, he has completed half of his Dīn, so let him fear Allāh regarding the other half." (Mishkāt)

In another Ḥadīth, the Holy Prophet ﷺ says addressing the youth,

يَا مَعْشَرَ الشَّبَابِ مَنِ اسْتَطَاعَ مِنْكُمُ الْبَاءَةَ فَلْيَتَزَوَّجْ فَإِنَّهُ أَغَضُّ لِلْبَصَرِ وَأَحْصَنُ لِلْفَرْجِ وَمَنْ لَمْ يَسْتَطِعْ فَعَلَيْهِ بِالصَّوْمِ فَإِنَّهُ لَهُ وِجَاءٌ

"O assembly of youth, the person who has the ability to get married (financially, physically), let him get married because this is a means

17

of his eyes and gaze being kept down. If he cannot, let him continuously fast because that will be a shield for him." (Bukhāri and Muslim)

Hence, Allāh has made this system whereby a person safeguards his chastity from evil things. When he wishes to fulfil his desires, he does so through lawful means i.e. marriage.

Allāh clearly states in the following verse:

فَمَنِ ابْتَغَى وَرَاءَ ذٰلِكَ فَأُولٰئِكَ هُمُ الْعَادُوْنَ

A person who searches for anything other than that (meaning the proper method), then they will be transgressing the limits. (23:7)

The verse above should be sufficient for a person to realise the true and proper way of fulfilling the desires, that is, through marriage.

This is why Allāh has said,

وَأَنْكِحُوا الْأَيَامٰى مِنْكُمْ وَالصَّالِحِيْنَ مِنْ عِبَادِكُمْ وَإِمَائِكُمْ إِنْ يَّكُوْنُوا فُقَرَاءَ يُغْنِهِمُ اللّٰهُ مِنْ فَضْلِه وَاللّٰهُ وَاسِعٌ عَلِيْمٌ

Get the unmarried ones among you married as well as those slave men and slave women who are righteous. If they are poor, then Allāh will make each of them independent by His Grace. Allāh is of ample means, All Knowing. (24:32)

Unfortunately, these days our youth think they are not ready. The question is, when will they be 'ready'? A Hadīth of the Holy Prophet ﷺ mentions,

If he becomes Bāligh (mature) and does not get married and he commits sin, then he will get sin and his parents will also get sin (Mishkāt). Innā lillāh.

There used to be a time when we used to think that a person should get married around the age of 16 or 17. But now, Subhān-Allāh, we have youngsters reaching the ages of 26 and 27, and they *still* feel 'it is not time yet'.

So respected readers, marriage should take place as quickly as possible, in order to preserve and save the chastity. Marriage becomes compulsory on a person when they know that they are going to fall into sins. May Allāh ﷻ protect our chastity and save us from all evils.

Āmīn.

Quality 5: Fulfilling Promises

وَالَّذِيْنَ هُمْ لِاَمٰنٰتِهِمْ وَعَهْدِهِمْ رَاعُوْنَ

And they who are to their trusts and their promises attentive (23:8)

The fifth quality of the pious—those who are the true believers—is that they fulfil their trusts. They ensure that the promises they make are fulfilled.

In this present time, we don't think much about this. In fact, many of us do not even realize when we have made a promise. Take for example, the student who joins the Madrasah for the first time. He is obliged to fill out an application form, in which he affirms that he will abide by the rules and regulations of that institute. The student should realise that this is also a promise. Hence, by breaking the codes of conduct relating to the Madrasah, is in reality breaking promises. Breaking promises are counted amongst major sins! We must realise this.

Punctuality is something which is always stipulated in employment contracts. If you are employed in a job, you are expected to arrive on time. If you arrive late, then you are breaking the terms of your contract. This counts as not fulfilling promises.

The UK, amongst many other countries, have numerous laws stipulated in regards to the roads. On the motorway, the limit is restricted to 70 mph. So when a person passes their driving test and begins to use the motorway, if they exceed this 70mph limit, they are breaking the law of the land. And in turn, they will be sinful in the eyes of Allāh ﷻ for breaking their promise.

This is an important point to stress. Any promise or pledge a person makes, whether that be regarding; the laws of the land, their employment, Madrasah or any organisation they are affiliated with, *must* be fulfilled. The agreement needs to be abided by, otherwise a person will be sinful for breaking their promise/agreement/trust. Of course, if there is a valid reason or emergency in which the agreement was violated, that is different.

To further emphasise the magnitude of breaking promises, let us ponder over the following Hadīth, where Rasūlullāh ﷺ describes this trait being amongst the signs of the hypocrite. Rasūlullāh ﷺ said:

آيَةُ الْمُنَافِقِ ثَلَاثٌ: إِذَا حَدَّثَ كَذَبَ، وإِذَا وَعَدَ أَخْلَفَ، وَإِذَا اتُّمِنَ خَانَ

(متفق عليه)

"Signs of a hypocrite are three: when he speaks; he lies, when he makes a promise; he breaks it and when he is given a trust; he goes against that trust." (Bukhāri and Muslim)

There is an incident mentioned in the books of Sīrah that occurred even before the Holy Prophet ﷺ received his Nabuwwat (prophethood). The Holy Prophet ﷺ and his friend, Abdullāh were taking part in a business transaction, whereby Abdullāh asked the Prophet ﷺ to wait for him at a certain place, and he would meet him there. Abdullāh did not meet the Holy Prophet ﷺ at the time stipulated, but returned after 3 days. To his surprise, he saw the Prophet ﷺ waiting there for him. Subhān-Allāh. The Holy Prophet ﷺ remained for three whole days because his friend had promised he would be coming.

Unfortunately, these important things tend to get overlooked in our day-to-day lives. During events, the host will stipulate a time, e.g. 1pm sharp. The question they will receive is, "Is that Asian time or English time?" Allāhu-Akbar. Never mind Asian or English time, this is the Islamic time! As Muslims, we need to fulfil our promises and pledges, and when we have given our word, we must abide by it.

A person may view these things as trivial but in reality, they are of great importance and do have consequences. We fail to take time seriously. We don't attend gatherings on time, so we don't manage to achieve other things in the time we have which leads us to devaluing time. When Subhān-Allāh, time is of the essence, it is the most valuable asset we hold.

If we were to simply acknowledge the Islamic system in regards to time, there is so much we could learn. All our activities are in tune with a particular system of time. Our five daily Salāh, each have their set times, which determine our schedule of that day.

In the Holy Qur'ān, Allāh ﷻ mentions:

$$إِنَّ الصَّلَاةَ كَانَتْ عَلَى الْمُؤْمِنِينَ كِتَابًا مَّوْقُوتًا$$

Indeed, prayer has been decreed upon the believers a decree of specified times. (4:103)

It is incumbent upon a believer to ensure that all of their promises; whether they are for Allāh ﷻ or the people, are fulfilled. A believer cannot say that they will work a 12 hour shift, then catch up with their five daily prayers when they finish. We would never adopt the same approach when it comes to our food, or anything else for that matter, so how can we consider such a negligent attitude with our Salāh? If anything, the promises we make to Allāh ﷻ should be of utmost importance, and we should not allow anything to come in the way of that.

When we were in عَالَمِ ارواح (the world of the souls) each and every one of us were asked by Allāh ﷻ "اَلَسْتُ بِرَبِّكُمْ" (Am I not your Lord?). To which we replied, "بَلٰیۡ شَهِدۡنَا" (Yes, we have testified.) This pledge we made with Allāh ﷻ in the Ālam-e-Arwāh must be fulfilled, for our own selves.

Financial dealings also fall under the category of promises. Many a times we see a person taking part in a business transaction, where they have taken the goods and promised to give the funds for the good the following day. In many cases, this 'tomorrow' never comes. From this we can marvel at the wise words of Sayyidunā 'Umar Fārūq ﷺ when he said, "You don't really know a person until you travel with him or do business with him." 'Safar' in the Arabic language is used for travel. In the literal sense, it means to illuminate. Where is the link between the common usage and the lexical? Well, when a person's character becomes illuminated, you begin to see their true habits and ways. This usually occurs when a person is engaged in financial dealings or travelling (Safar).

May Allāh ﷻ make us among those who can truly keep their promises in all instances. Āmīn!

Quality 6: Salāh

وَالَّذِيْنَ هُمْ عَلٰى صَلَوَاتِهِمْ يُحَافِظُوْنَ

And they who carefully maintain their prayers (23:9)

Subhān-Allāh, the first quality mentioned by Allāh ﷻ was Salāh and again, He is reminding us of it towards the end. This further emphasises the importance of such an act which we *must* take care of, in order to be truly successful. The first time Allāh ﷻ mentioned Salāh in the Sūrah was in regards to the Khushū. Over here, Allāh ﷻ turns our attention to another fundamental quality, punctuality.

Salāh is absolutely essential in the life of a believer. It is loved by Allāh ﷻ so much, that He made it obligatory upon a Muslim. Allāh ﷻ does not want us to miss our Salāh, hence, He has stipulated severe punishment if we are to miss it. In a Hadīth al-Qudsī, Allāh ﷻ mentions the superiority of the Farā'idh acts.

The Messenger of Allāh ﷺ said, "Allāh, the Exalted, has said: 'I will declare war against him who treats with hostility a pious worshipper of Mine. And the most beloved thing with which My slave comes nearer to Me, is what I have enjoined upon him; and My slave keeps on coming closer to Me through performing Nawāfil (voluntary prayers or doing extra deeds besides what is obligatory) until I love him, (so much so that) I become his hearing with which he hears, and his sight with which he sees, and his hand with which he strikes, and his leg with which he walks; and if he asks Me something, I will surely give him, and if he seeks My Protection (refuge), I will surely protect him". (Bukhāri)

Subhān-Allāh. We can understand the reality of Farā'idh acts such as Salāh just by reading this divine utterance. The punishment of missing Salāh is not to be taken lightly. The Holy Qur'ān mentions an incident whereby the people of Paradise will ask the people of the Fire "مَا سَلَكَكُمْ فِي سَقَرَ؟" ("What put you into Saqar?"). Saqar is one of the names of Jahannam. They will say, "لَمْ نَكُ مِنَ الْمُصَلِّيْنَ" ("We were not of those who prayed").

We can now understand why it is said:

فَرْقُ بَيْنَ الْمَرْءِ وِ الْكُفْرِ تَرْكُ الصَّلَاةِ

The difference between a person and Kufr is the missing of Salāh.

Allāhu-Akbar, the one who neglects his Salāh will ultimately fall in the ditch of Kufr. Hence, Salāh must not be neglected. It will only lead to our destruction and failure. This is why it is repeated within the qualities of the successful.

Reward of the Successful

For those who fulfil all the requirements mentioned previously, of Salāh, Zakāt, chasity, fulfilment of promises and avoiding futile things, Allāh ﷻ has promised:

$$أُولٰئِكَ هُمُ الْوَارِثُوْنَ$$
Those are the inheritors (23:10)

The inheritors of what? One may ask. Well, the best thing a person can ever inherit, Jannah!

$$اَلَّذِيْنَ يَرِثُوْنَ الْفِرْدَوْسَ هُمْ فِيْهَا خَالِدُوْنَ$$
who will inherit al-Firdaus. They will abide therein eternally. (23:11)

The successful will not inherit just any Paradise. Rather, they will inherit the highest rank of Jannah, that is, Jannatul Firdaus! What a lofty station and great reward. Subhān-Allāh.

Why does Allāh use the word 'inheritance'. Consider the following scenario in order to understand. A person when his father passes away, will surely inherit from his father's assets and nobody can deprive him of that. Meaning, that it is a divine order of Allāh ﷻ. If somebody takes that away, they will be doing gross injustice to that person.

So in regards to those mentioned in - ٱلَّذِيْنَ يَرِثُوْنَ الْفِرْدَوْسَ - they are those people who will inherit Jannatul Firdaus which will never be taken away from them.

We have reached the end of the 6 qualities of the successful, Alhamdulillāh. May Allāh ﷻ give us all the ability and Tawfīq to act on these qualities in the true sense, inculcating them diligently in our lives. May Allāh ﷻ make us truly successful, in this life and the Hereafter, Āmīn.

رَبَّنَآ آتِنَا فِي الدُّنْيَا حَسَنَةً وَّفِي الْآخِرَةِ حَسَنَةً وَّقِنَا عَذَابَ النَّارِ

"Our Lord, give us in this world (that which is) good and in the Hereafter (that which is) good and protect us from the punishment of the Fire." (2:201)

Kanzul Bāri

Kanzul Bāri provides a detailed commentary of the Ahādeeth contained in Saheeh al-Bukhāri. The commentary includes Imām Bukhāri's ﷺ biography, the status of his book, spiritual advice, inspirational accounts along with academic discussions related to Fiqh, its application and differences of opinion. Moreover, it answers objections arising in one's mind about certain Ahādeeth. Inquisitive students of Hadeeth will find this commentary a very useful reference book in the final year of their Ālim course for gaining a deeper understanding of the science of Hadeeth. **UK RRP: £15.00**

How to Become a Friend of Allāh ﷺ

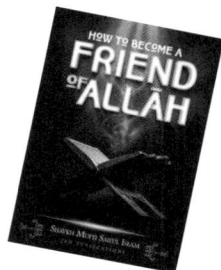

The friends of Allāh ﷺ have been described in detail in the Holy Qur'ān and Āhadeeth. This book endeavours its readers to help create a bond with Allāh ﷺ in attaining His friendship as He is the sole Creator of all material and immaterial things. It is only through Allāh's ﷺ friendship, an individual will achieve happiness in this life and the Hereafter, hence eliminate worries, sadness, depression, anxiety and misery of this world. **UK RRP:**

Gems & Jewels

This book contains a selection of articles which have been gathered for the benefit of the readers covering a variety of topics on various aspects of daily life. It offers precious advice and anecdotes that contain moral lessons. The advice captivates its readers and will extend the narrowness of their thoughts to deep reflection, wisdom and appreciation of the purpose of our existence. **UK RRP: £4.00**

End of Time

This book is a comprehensive explanation of the three Sūrahs of Juzz Amma; Sūrah Takweer, Sūrah Infitār and Sūrah Mutaffifeen. This book is a continuation from the previous book of the same author, 'Horrors of Judgement Day'. The three Sūrahs vividly sketch out the scene of the Day of Judgement and describe the state of both the inmates of Jannah and Jahannam. Mufti Saiful Islām Sāhib provides an easy but comprehensive commentary of the three Sūrahs facilitating its understanding for the readers whilst capturing the horrific scene of the ending of the world and the conditions of mankind on that horrific Day. **UK RRP: £5.00**

Golden Legacy of Spain

Andalus (modern day Spain), the long lost history, was once a country that produced many great calibre of Muslim scholars comprising of Mufassirūn, Muhaddithūn, Fuqahā, judges, scientists, philosophers, surgeons, to name but a few. The Muslims conquered Andalus in 711 AD and ruled over it for eight-hundred years. This was known as the era of Muslim glory. Many non-Muslim Europeans during that time travelled to Spain to study under Muslim scholars. The remanences of the Muslim rule in Spain are manifested through their universities, magnificent palaces and Masājid carved with Arabic writings, standing even until today. In this book, Shaykh Mufti Saiful Islām shares some of his valuable experiences he witnessed during his journey to Spain. **UK RRP: £3.00**

Ideal Youth

This book contains articles gathered from various social media avenues; magazines, emails, WhatsApp and telegram messages that provide useful tips of advice for those who have the zeal to learn and consider changing their negative habits and behavior and become better Muslims to set a positive trend for the next generation. **UK RRP:£4:00**

Ideal Teacher

This book contains abundance of precious advices for the Ulamā who are in the teaching profession. It serves to present Islamic ethical principles of teaching and to remind every teacher of their moral duties towards their students. This book will Inshā-Allāh prove to be beneficial for newly graduates and scholars wanting to utilize their knowledge through teaching. **UK RRP:£4:00**

Ideal Student

This book is a guide for all students of knowledge in achieving the excellent qualities of becoming an ideal student. It contains precious advices, anecdotes of our pious predecessors and tips in developing good morals as a student. Good morals is vital for seeking knowledge. A must for all students if they want to develop their Islamic Knowledge. **UK RRP:£4:00**

Ideal Parents

This book contains a wealth of knowledge in achieving the qualities of becoming ideal parents. It contains precious advices, anecdotes of our pious predecessors and tips in developing good parenthood skills. Good morals is vital for seeking knowledge. A must for all parents . **UK RRP:£4:00**

Ideal Couple

This book is a compilation of inspiring stories and articles containing useful tips and life skills for every couple. Marriage life is a big responsibility and success in marriage is only possible if the couple know what it means to be an ideal couple. **UK RRP:£4:00**

Ideal Role Model

This book is a compilation of sayings and accounts of our pious predecessors. The purpose of this book is so we can learn from our pious predecessors the purpose of this life and how to attain closer to the Creator. Those people who inspires us attaining closeness to our Creator are our true role models. A must everyone to read. **UK RRP:£4:00**

Bangladesh– A Land of Natural Beauty

This book is a compilation of our respected Shaykh's journeys to Bangladesh including visits to famous Madāris and Masājid around the country. The Shaykh shares some of his thought provoking experiences and his personal visits with great scholars in Bangladesh. **UK RRP: £4.00**

Pearls from the Qur'an

This series begins with the small Sūrahs from 30th Juzz initially, unravelling its heavenly gems, precious advices and anecdotes worthy of personal reflection. It will most definitely benefit both those new to as well as advanced students of the science of Tafsīr. The purpose is to make it easily accessible for the general public in understanding the meaning of the Holy Qur'ān. **UK RRP: £10.00**

When the Heavens Split

This book contains the commentary of four Sūrahs from Juzz Amma namely; Sūrah Inshiqāq, Sūrah Burūj, Sūrah Tāriq and Sūrah A'lā. The first two Sūrahs contain a common theme of capturing the scenes and events of the Last Day and how this world will come to an end. However, all four Sūrahs mentioned, have a connection of the journey of humanity, reflection on nature, how nature changes and most importantly, giving severe warnings to mankind about the punishments and exhorting them to prepare for the Hereafter through good deeds and refraining from sins. **UK RRP: £4.00**

The Lady who Spoke the Qur'ān

The Holy Prophet ﷺ was sent as a role model who was the physical form of the Holy Qur'ān. Following the ways of the Holy Prophet ﷺ in every second of our lives is pivotal for success. This booklet tells us the way to gain this success. It also includes an inspirational incident of an amazing lady who only spoke from the Holy Qur'an throughout her life. We will leave it to our readers to marvel at her intelligence, knowledge and piety expressed in this breath-taking episode. **UK RRP:£3:00**

Dearest Act to Allāh

Today our Masājid have lofty structures, engraved brickworks, exquisite chandeliers and laid rugs, but they are spiritually deprived due to the reason that the Masājid are used for social purposes including backbiting and futile talk rather than the performance of Salāh, Qur'ān recitation and the spreading of true authentic Islamic knowledge. This book elaborates on the etiquettes of the Masjid and the importance of Salāh with Quranic and prophetic proofs along with some useful anecdotes to emphasize their importance. **UK RRP:£3:00**

Don't Delay Your Nikāh

Marriage plays an important role in our lives. It is a commemoration of the union of two strangers who will spend the rest of their remaining lives with one another. Marriage ought to transpire comfort and tranquillity whereby the couple share one another's sorrow and happiness. It is strongly recommended that our brothers and sisters read and benefit from this book and try to implement it into our daily lives in order to once more revive the Sunnah of the Holy Prophet ﷺ on such occasions and repel the prevalent sins and baseless customs.

UK RRP:£3:00

Miracle of the Holy Qur'ān

The scholars of Islām are trying to wake us all up, however, we are busy dreaming of the present world and have forgotten our real destination. Shaykh Mufti Saiful Islām Sāhib has been conducted Tafsīr of the Holy Qur'ān every week for almost two decades with the purpose of reviving its teachings and importance. This book is a transcription of two titles; Miracle of the Holy Qur'ān and The Revelation of the Holy Qur'ān, both delivered during the weekly Tafsīr sessions. **UK RRP:£3:00**

You are what you Eat

Eating Halāl and earning a lawful income plays a vital role in the acceptance of all our Ibādāt (worship) and good deeds. Mufti Saiful Islām Sāhib has presented a discourse on this matter in one of his talks. I found the discourse to be very beneficial, informative and enlightening on the subject of Halāl and Harām that clarifies its importance and status in Islām. I strongly recommend my Muslim brothers and sisters to read this treatise and to study it thoroughly.

UK RRP:£3:00

Sleepers of the Cave

The Tafsīr of Sūrah Kahf is of crucial importance in this unique and challenging time we are currently living in. This book is evidently beneficial for all Muslims, more crucial for the general public. This is because Mufti Sāhib gives us extensive advice on how to act accordingly when treading the path of seeking knowledge. Readers will find amazing pieces of advice in terms of etiquettes regarding seeking knowledge and motivation, Inshā-Allāh. **UK RRP:£5:00**

Contentment of the Heart

The purification of the soul and its rectification are matters of vital importance which were brought by our Holy Prophet e to this Ummah. The literal meaning of Tazkiyah is 'to cleanse'. The genuine Sūfis assert that the foundation and core of all virtuous character is sincerity and the basis for all evil characteristics and traits is love for this world. This book endeavors to address certain spiritual maladies and how to overcome them using Islamic principles. **UK RRP:£5:00**

Contemporary Fiqh

This book is a selection of detailed *Fiqhi* (juridical) articles on contemporary legal issues. These detailed articles provide an in depth and elaborative response to some of the queries posted to us in our Fatawa department over the last decade. The topics discussed range between purity, domestic issues, Halāl and Harām, Islamic medical ethics, marital issues, rituals and so forth. Many of the juristic cases are unprecedented as a result of the ongoing societal changes and newly arising issues. **UK RRP:£6:00**

Ideal Society

In this book, 'Ideal Society' which is a commentary of Sūrah Hujurāt, Shaykh Mufti Saiful Islām Sāhib explains the lofty status of our beloved Prophet 🕌, the duties of the believers and general mankind and how to live a harmonious social life, which is free from evil, jealousy and vices. Inshā-Allāh, this book will enable and encourage the readers to adopt a social life which will ultimately bring happiness and joy to each and every individual.

UK RRP:£5:00